ADAPTATIONS

ADAPTATIONS

POEMS

VA Smith

GREEN WRITERS PRESS | Brattleboro, Vermont

Printed in the United States.

10 9 8 7 6 5 4 3 2 1

Green Writers Press is a Vermont-based publisher whose mission is to
spread a message of hope and renewal through the words and images we
publish. Throughout we will adhere to our commitment to preserving and
protecting the natural resources of the earth. To that end, a percentage of
our proceeds will be donated to environmental and social-activist groups.
Green Writers Press gratefully acknowledges support from individual
donors, friends, and readers to help support the environment and our
publishing initiative.

Giving Voice to Writers & Artists Who Will Make the World a Better Place
Green Writers Press | Brattleboro, Vermont
www.greenwriterspress.com

ISBN: 979-8-9914134-7-3

COVER IMAGES: ISTOCKPHOTO

For Sue Barney Mathias—
poetry aficionado, beautiful being,
ardent, lifelong friend.

"Let us remember ... that in the end we go to poetry for one reason, so that we might more fully inhabit our lives and the world in which we live them, and that if we more fully inhabit these things, we might be less apt to destroy both."

CHRISTIAN WYMAN

CONTENTS

I

II

III

IV

On Evolutionary Adaptability:
  A Chthulucene Sonnet Crown

I

WAVE FIELD

Maya Lin's acre of waves
brings ocean to earth, sculpted
from soil, grass seed, into

seven rows of undulation.
When we stand on a hill
above them, the billows

rotate as we walk in
a circle, green swells
not yet blued with late

afternoon shadow. We
wonder aloud that bare
March will whip gray waves,

that January will roil frothy,
frost-capped mounds.
I think of Homer tossing

Odysseus against the waves
for a decade, onto
Calypso's witchy sphere,

then battered against Scylla.
Or the American Homer,
Winslow, watercoloring

waves, icy fierceness tearing
rock-studded Maine coasts.
If we descend into

these waves, they will cup
our bodies into their silent
curves with the lie

of lullaby. If we nestle
there to picnic, the waves
will whisper what we

have made of earth, oceans:
a tomb, its door nearly closed,
demanding that we decide.

HOW I DREAM ABOUT CLIMATE CHANGE

Giant neon tetras, angelfish,
blue tangs tacked to tree trunks
like installation art. Shining,
they open and close their mouths
in rhythm. Eyes panicked, are they
astonished to find themselves
suspended, stuck in air—
their miraculous, new medium?

I may be anthropomorphizing.

I have been chosen to witness
and to rescue, to return
tropical fish to watery,
glistening health, enliven
coral reefs' bone-white graves.

In waking life, I massage
sockeye salmon with miso,
commune with this piece
of blood-orange flesh,
welcome it to tonight's feast.
I admire out loud its Alaskan
source, its green rating. True,
I would rather it came to me
whole, head and body intact,
like the oily sardines I fed on

in Portugal, grilled with lemon,
served as a slender tribe.

Flashing silver streams of motion
near oceans' surface, sardine schools
replenish by billions for eons, too busy,
frankly, to signify danger in dreams.

I may be anthropomorphizing.

EACH OTHER

I rake rooftop beds,
pull wrinkled red berries

through soil loosened
by vermiculite, wind.

This is the season
of crossings: sun South

to North, Hellebores nodding,
pale pods opening

to baby pink faces.
Cindy's thin face looked

wind-whipped when I found
her that deep winter night

walking her dog on our street,
a pause from her cat's dying

shrieks, her friend's ZOOM
funeral the following day.

This month's brunch at her
house she showed me a photo

of her future puppy, still
in utero, due in April,

its brown umbilical cord
crawling north like a worm.

I bend to snip dried
mum stalks and bloom,

stroke their soft undergrowth.
Cindy never wanted

children. My eggs run dry,
I dream I'm pregnant with

babies, puppies, kittens.
Another living loop I crave.

Often, my newborns
disintegrate—then

I carry night mourning
into the day. Some stay

whole, latch to my nipple,
our birth-wet faces

saucers we offer each
other, licking, lapping.

PEACHES

In Richmond's Fan District,
June Farmers' Market features
furry Georgia peaches mounding
in cardboard boxes, crowding
Crayola-bright sweet peppers,
baby cukes, inevitable

zucchini. My friend and I
cannot not see these fruits
as Cézanne saw them, graceful
globes never falling, never
blemished or eaten. Who would
fault us? We are not naïve

aesthetes, precious hoarders
of Grecian Urn "Nevers,"
but best pals since high school,
one trapped in sorrow like her
caged son, imprisoned, the other
holding her own against brain

cancer. She's stuck on buying
the bargain bushel but her
husband will not house all those
peaches & he's hidden her
bankcard, her brain begging her,
he claims, to overspend.

"They'll just rot in our fruit basket,"
he wagers. Perhaps. But we crave
juice & joy from this fruit: pies
cooling, oozing orange syrup,
tomatoes sliced with basil &
peaches, chicken grilled with

stone fruit, brushed with balsamic.
I buy the peaches, see lapis
blue bowls in her kitchen toppling
with smudges of pink, yellow
& rouge. My love: how can you not
feel abnormal cells dividing then

multiplying in your brain, sense
daily the thin blade between living
& rotting? My darling: let me
massage your feet & neck like
a comfort woman, feed you
ripe red raspberries, one by

one, like tart kisses.

BEFORE I KNEW ABOUT BREAKFAST AT TIFFANY'S

That sixties summer my family swam Moon River most days, our strokes
across water wider than a mile among tributaries crisscrossing

our tiny house and yard   streaming through
a confluence of song   buoying us

            with shared possibility:

my quiet brother   sailing our porch-swing
crooning to his crush   *You Dream Maker, You Heartbreaker,*
to her blonde braids
and lavish dimples

lyrics calling me   from my new aqua transistor,
as I freestyle,   to drift with mystery—
                            "*Wherever you're going,*
                            I'm going your way"—
       then side stroke to Dad floating through the living room like
                            a Chagall lover cradling
                            our *Moon River* LP

like Andy Williams
with his clean haircut
piercing blue eyes,
long nose, bright smile—   Dad echoes Mr. Williams tenor, too,

11

so for that summer   though our father mixes chemicals
                            at a paper mill
it seems our family
becomes *The Andy Williams Show*,
just by living at home,   *Moon River* takes us everywhere.

ARIA TO MY GLASSES

A white triangle kite sails a beach blue sky,
            light and water bouncing each other,
rinsing the day of subtlety. I am simply glad.

I have not immersed myself this summer
            though I'm pulled today toward
Atlantic waves, drifting in their rise before

ducking under to secret, salty cold. I still
            wonder why I kept my glasses on
as if they were a part of me, attached living

matter allowing me to see. A big one flattens
            me before I can save them,
rolls me into its briny cyclone, spins me,

abrades me. Nothing personal, I know.
            My glasses have gone to sea.
Still, I crawl the shoreline in lacy foam

like the baby beside me, as if we are playing,
            glopping sand piles together.
When I concede that the ocean's got them,

I see bottle-nosed dolphins tossing them
            in keep away, my glasses'
arms skittering across the ocean floor

like spindly crab legs. I picture a mermaid
         idling on a rocky crag,
her tail a wave of green shimmer, my glasses

perched on her sun-scrubbed nose. She sees
         the ocean piled with microplastics,
   diapers, hypodermic needles, crammed with cans,

condoms, Legos, Barbies and buckets.
      Anthropocene flotsam floating
across Earth's oceans for a brief forever.

MOON JELLIES

It's true that behind this glass
aquarium flooded with deep

space blue, they look like moons,
more beautiful, surely, than

spinning in ocean's gray churn,
waves slamming their soft strokes,

stomping the shimmery
shimmy of their bodies'

luminescence. Why should
I walk away? Tropical Debby

storms outside. Inside my
raincoat pocket waits a fat,

veggie wrap. And those shark
tanks beside me don't glitter

with the thrill of safe danger
they once offered when my

sons' kindergarten hands
found mine. So I just watch

the jellies being in this
glass box of night sky sea.

Bell-shaped bodies float without
heart, brain or lungs. Their

transparent cores cover four
gleaming gonads. Pulsating

white parasols trail a crown
of gluey tentacles

flowering with stinging cells.
I see them zap plankton,

lift them to their anus/mouths
with tea party delicacy.

I'm tired of solidity.
Peel wax paper from

my sandwich. Swallow
spinach soggy with spread,

turning fast to green algae.
Mindlessly, a milky mass

without sight or breathe, I
tumble, joy-throb from myself.

UKRAINIAN EASTER EGGS

There in our snug living
room, a TV tray her craft
center, my seventies mom
laughed at *Carol Burnett,*

*M*A*S*H*, All in the Family,*
her pop cult cover for pysanky
witchery, gently pricking a hole
with her needle at egg's two tips,

blowing never-to-be chicks
into a bowl for scrambling,
then focusing her gaze,
heating her kiska over candle

flame, drawing beeswax lines,
mixing arcadia and pagan hex signs—
eight-point stars, arrowed branches,
verdure munching cottontails—

with crucifixion, Golgotha crosses.
These marks would be shell white,
pure—then dipping eggs into scarlet,
sapphire, the purple of resurrection,

her folk-art palimpsests of death
and spring, paeans to sun gods,

to the Son as God. Episcopal
Sundays aside, mom sensed

what Egyptians, Greeks, Romans
believed: the universe emerged
from a mother's egg. Let's leave
her here: a decade before Ukraine

broke free from Soviet's Union,
30 years after Babi Yar, 50 before
Russia would bomb Kyiv, Mariupol,
Kharkov, when pysanky will

scatter streets with silt, shattered
fine as bone.

CHAOS THEORY

Watch me bathe myself in the cool
blues, grays, and sages of the living
room I have filled with muted
leathers, nubby wool rugs,
a quiet flow of Carrara marble
over mantel and counter.

When his stainless-steel bowl flies
into the refrigerator, bounces cole-
slaw across the floor, confettis
cabinets with cabbage, my eyes
close to Yo-Yo Ma bowing Bach's
Cello Sonata in G Minor Prelude,
open to shut Mary Oliver's
Dream Work.

I have havened home against
addiction, bi-polarities political
and chemical, democracies and
partner promises that lean toward
falling, failing.

Slipping from chaos, I fast walk
intervals into October's pumpkined
light, Earth's axis tilting predictable
degrees further from our sun,
its shards shimmering through giant
maples, sturdy pines, feigning safety,
order.

ON VISITING MY YOUNGEST SON
IN A STATE CORRECTIONAL INSTITUTE

I only know concertina wire from TV until I park
at prison, barbed silver circles scrolling skyline,
slicing clouds, twinkling on this moist, New Year's
morning. Primary colors slash every snack-strewn
surface of the meeting room, where multi-hued men
in brown zipped jumpsuits appear like uniformed
grade schoolers on Parents' Day, eager boys eating
crackers, sharing artwork. My son and I meet on
either side of a poly-glass partition, speak through
wall phones and tension, then sink, finally, into regret's
worn sofa. I listen to him talk about substance abuse
classes, court-ordered, writing intensive. I pretend he's
a college client I coach to develop textured paragraphs,
telling verbs, sentence transitions.

HISTORY WITH JEHOVAH'S WITNESSES

Clustered outside the ShopRite most days, draped in
no-nonsense dark fabric, they smile and nod each time
I take their *Watchtower* pamphlet. I am mesmerized by
the dozens of tiny bodies, black as licorice nibs, without
faces or clothes, caught up in the Rapture, spinning, arms
akimbo, appearing to climb if not crawl or claw their way
heavenward. These are drawn in sepia, signal serious End
Times, though my Episcopalian grandmother and mother
smirk at me as they test the tomatoes, reach for a blood-
ied roast wrapped in plastic. I turn the pages of this holy
comic book, worry that my family might not rise together.
Worse, would I even make the cut? My mid-years find me
hiding behind curtains, in corners, as they ring my doorbell
to transform me, long a secular smart ass, eye-rolling my
way through the Nicene Creed at funerals. Last week some
Witnesses and I meet on my street, them climbing my
neighbor's stoop, me walking my hound, he lifting his leg
on every post and twig, while one of the women croons,
"That's right, do your morning business, honey! What a
good boy!" I walk on, find myself missing them, as if they
are already ascending together.

MOTHER NEVER SMOKED

Though half her Bridge Club
killed a pack each day.
We drew delight from
Bridge Night Prep: ladling
bridge mix & butter mints
into the cupped palms
of silver bowls, pressing
pale blue linens, polishing
heirloom forks & spoons.
I'd anticipate my dance through
spirals of blue smoke genies
as I cleared plates crumbed
with pie crust, emptied ashtrays,
their scattered butts kissed
with lipstick.

This charm reversed by
age sixteen, my bedroom feet
from what sounded like canned
laughter as I opened *Malcolm X's*
Autobiography, dropped the needle
on Mama Cass, Grace Slick, to drown
Bridge Club chatter. I'd dream
of California on a winter's day,
or one pill that might make me larger,
then swipe bridge cigarettes, steal
to my woods, practice my exhale
in silent darkness.

By this century Mother
laughed at herself in assisted
living, calling out *Bingo!*,
relieved from bidding stress.
She joked about bags of chips,
game prizes she'd foist on visitors.
Together we served ladies
coffee & pie again, their husbands
dead, smokers trailing oxygen
from walkers & wheelchairs,
mother's bridge tables & silver
service sold at auction.

Maria lights a twiggy doobie
over my marble counter, Burgundy,
& Brie. I perform my own rite,
lift on tiptoes to grab the bridge
ashtray, last of the Seventies set,
a 4″ x 4″ glass square
like a miniature card table,
indentations for cigarettes
like curved mid-century chairs
I want to make larger
& land on, Jefferson Airplane
flying us, the smoke a snaking,
purple haze.

II

WHEN HAYDEN CARRUTH VISITED MY HIGH SCHOOL CREATIVE WRITING CLASS

it was the end of the last
century. I was the teacher,
inches older than my students,
their faces studded with piercings
and zits, declaring in hushed
voices their longing to become
poets.

Legends came to us, largesse
from our local college's
Poetry Center: Maxine Kumin,
wearing an athletic, equine
grace, talked to the teens about
poetry of place, her New Hampshire,
read about moose scat, landlocked
seas of violets.

Carolyn Kizer, trailing whiffs
of screw-you glamour, enacted
her "from Sappho to myself,"
her *Pro Femina*, warning the girls
how the boys ruled poetry's empire,
guarded its gates.

Galway Kinnell, all denim
and tweed, read "After Making

Love We Hear Footsteps," muted
Irish brogue caressing the phrase
"cum-cry," kids later trying
that trope on for weeks.

I don't recall what Hayden
Carruth read. Grizzled, medicated,
maybe, with the old stuff that
wrung wildness from the brain.
He talked of madness, of the desire
not to be, of a Thanksgiving
dinner baked with sorrow. He said,
"These things, too, will happen
to you." His eyes searched ours
for darkness. Students bent their heads.
I joined his gaze, offered: "I don't know
how to thank you."

HIGH ROCK HIKING

Bare white birch branches poke
skyward like O'Keefe's
antlers framing blue eternity.

This is not her desert
grassland. No piñon pine
needles to soften our steps,

though cedar woodfire
sweeps our way as we walk
the red trailhead. Pennsylvania

root and rock sculpt our climb
to more majestic stone. It's hot
this early October. We stop

for water, mind measure
the creek gully receding
below us. A surprise to hear,

this high, water's rush while
land's this dry. Yet hurricanes
flood Gulf Coasts as we hike,

smash inland further north,
flatten tucked-in mountain towns.
I want to stop counting

the worlds and my daily dead.
Yet this lookout proffers elegy.
A shrine appears at our feet,

talismans scattered about,
naming the dead: *RIP, Tanner*
inked on poster board.

In photos collaged, framed,
Tanner throws a younger boy
through the air. In the next,

both land in the bright splash
of a pool. In another,
Tanner kisses a girl.

Leans out a car window,
leather jacket, James Dean shot.
Around this altar, remnants

of his young life, curated:
mirrored white sunglasses,
license plate, nubby orange

Varsity letter. I study the dive
he may have made below,
how rock would break it,

and him. Imagine Tanner
swimming in air,
perfectly alive.

ELEGY FOR A MAJORETTE

The morning that is your last,
I make breakfast for your family,
peel avocados' pebbled skin from
flesh flashing a green that hurts.
Your sons, now fathers, slide egg yolk
like sunrise over seeded toast,
recall after-school cookies still warm
from your oven. They speak of the new
stage to be named for you as I move
to your stillness in the living room
hospital bed. Your succulent in the window
wrinkles with water's lack, your coral
t-shirt dampens your breasts, your breathing
steadies, measured with morphine.
I kiss your forehead, rest my mouth
on the moist field of your skin, look
past your theatres, cities, decades:
back to the West Village's No Name Bar
where we danced on tables sticky with beer,
back to our hometown parades, football game
halftimes, your tanned, shapely legs alive
with kicks and struts, your fingers twirling
figure eights like magic tricks, your eyes then,
as now, wide and blue with beyond.

GRINDAVÍK, ICELAND

June days that never night,
we bike at midnight through
sun and wind to the harbor,

walk with care across shiny
basalt rocks to the salting
station, carry the slit cod

stacked like fine, cotton aprons
to the largest stones, bend
to flatten their salty, sopping

flesh to dry in sunshine.
I story my sister about
Ràn, our goddess planting

whales into water, providing
salty beneficence. When we
rest, Anna opens her purse,

pours krónur into her palm
saying: "Fish is work, Asta,
only that." Not for me.

When wind's up, I pretend
I might sail the fish triangles
I hold to Norway, or fly them

high, like white kites. My sister
shivers when wet needles prick
our faces. I say, *Your cod could*

be a folded umbrella. Open
it against this rain! Fish are slippery,
Anna—an entire universe.

I HAVE NOT BEEN ABLE TO WRITE
THE LAKE ONTARIO POEM

I knew I'd seen this lake at least twice before that summer.
Once as a kid with my parents on the Canadian side of
Niagara Falls. I'd left my faux alligator pocketbook on a
tourist trolly roving the Falls' manicured green park. This
lost purse held a Canadian Mounted Police charm for my
bracelet, bought with my allowance. He was dressed, I
remember thinking, like those Buckingham Palace guards
I'd seen on TV, though mine was smaller than a paper clip.
We left my name and address at the Niagara Falls Lost
& Found. I'd lost something, it seemed, I would never
get back. But damn—it arrived months later in the mail,
wrapped in brown paper, the address crisscrossed with all
kinds of important seeming, international stickers. And
damn—that silver Mountie, who was not on a horse, was
tucked inside the zip pocket of my recovered, rectangle bag.

Decades later I gave a conference paper in Toronto, some-
thing relating to women writers and otherness, and after-
ward, seated high on a hotel bar stool, flirting with a man
not my husband, I turned to cross my legs and saw Lake
Ontario from a wall of windows, moonlight making its
waver and weave sexy.

But this summer Lake Ontario was different. Or I was. As
we walked my friend's tony Toronto suburb, the lake flashed
around every turn, defining this breezy July afternoon like

an archetype. Driving me later to my Airbnb, my girl
Allie and I got out, snuck quietly, hidden, like the time we
smoked weed outside the Philadelphia Museum of Art,
behind the bushes. We were secretive this time, too.

Twilight laid blue webbing across the backyards of wealth,
those low-slung, understated architectures of the house-
on-the-water rich. We were there for something unspoken,
sneaking to witness a gloaming moment, trespassing on
private property for stolen loveliness. Or the Great Lake's
blessing. We trod lightly over pebbled walkways, lit low
by rows of domed lights. Lushness sounded from waves
washing rocks. Everywhere was hush and glow. Allie re-
peated as she led, "Just wait, there's more," but I wanted to
stand still and cry. Even to die. I guess numinosity found
me, pouring an ache deep as the lake. So even now, this
poem shifts, rounds the corner, slips away.

HOW TO MAKE JANUARY

And who would not—
following a month
of feasting and fests
drowned in eggnog,
wassail, candled tables
groaning with short
bovine rib, sweet crustacean
meat, wreaths of cheesy bread,
circles of sour creamed latkes—

devote themselves to
winter's delicate broths?

Begin a new year with
chicken soup, that fowl's
skeleton boiled with bouquet
of thyme and sage,
fresh stock simmered
with onion and carrots
to cleanse sinus and throat,
silky noodles stirred
with shredded bird breast
and thigh.

Mid-month, mark the creeping
back of light. Stew pink lentils
in full-fat coconut milk,

add sweet potato rounds,
red curry paste—sun's
striations in motion.

Celebrate January's last
days with Italian Wedding Soup,
marriage of poultry and leaf—
small meatballs, baby spinach,
ditalini's tiny tubes swimming
in parsleyed broth—a summer
tease.

So who would not welcome
what soup makes us know?
Elegance of budgets, bare
trees, fearful scarcity
of January snow.

CASSEROLE

I am standing at counter's edge,
              snapping florets from broccoli's thick
              stalk, tossing green glory into the sink's
              colander, watering tiny trees.
I praise how cooking washes me clean.

I am making a covered dish for the family
              of a friend, a mother, at 50, struck silent,
              no movement, a stroke. For a month no
              kiss has awakened her. I picture her tween
              and teen, Snapchat Hansel and Gretel,
              foraging on Door Dash, her husband leaving
              for work as they sleep among the crumbs.
 I worry their house's quiet will scream like their mother's
silence.

I am simmering brown rice with shallots and broth,
              mixing soft starch with milk, cheddar.
              I want to stretch this recipe for Esperanza,
              Honduran attorney turned house cleaner,
              running from the cartel, waiting years
              for asylum, sharing two bedrooms with her
              daughters, her brother and his family, eating
              from their shared pot of desperation.
I tell this dish histories, how few leave home unless they must.

I am slicing cutlets from a bird breast to poach in wine,
          wanting to loaves and fishes this
          dish, make mounds and then planes full,
          fly food to Haiti, to the children in the streets
          hiding from gangs, themselves kids with
          machine guns, who are also hungry.
          I want to offer breasts to their mouths,
          wipe their dirty faces, bend to bathe their feet.
I show this skillet a map, trace this country's proximity to
my own.

I am layering broccoli and rice, chicken and cheesy cream,
          in a blasted bowl the size of Gaza,
          where after 20 million pounds of
          US aid entered that strip's pier,
          it was dismantled. Today, innocents
          without arms, legs or parents must
          stop running for safety, know no
          shelter remains. To live they must
          sort through rubble mixed with
          frayed flesh, American-made
          bombs, torn pita, my free-range
          chicken, a strict, ethical choice.
Shame stains my white kitchen counter. I watch it spread.

CARAVAGGIO'S LIGHTBOX

Because I waver whether
to read uncanny
coincidence as signs
from the universe

when two separate
sources in one day
cite Caravaggio's
darkness lit electrically.

Because I leap to a woo-woo
yes, I whisk back decades
to Florence, a relentless
forced march through

dozens of museums, duomos,
while a husband chased
Baroque art gloom.

Because I good-girl
studied Caravaggio's
Medusa, Bacchus,
The Sacrifice of Isaac,

content falling on
infanticide, chiaroscuro

leaning heavily
toward darkness.

Because gasping for
air and light, I found
Uffizi's Botticelli gallery,
faced the giant *Birth of Venus,*

goddess perched on the bivalve
that birthed her, a scalloped
pedestal echoing the pale
peach of her newborn

woman's flesh, ocean waves
repeated in the long loops
of golden hair swirling
across her breast, meeting
at the mound of her namesake.
Because pastel lushness
everywhere, gynocentric
as fuck, fit exactly
my fin de siècle feminism.

Because Botticelli's
clarity now invites
my yawn, I turn to
Caravaggio's *Sleeping*

Cupid on my laptop,
its dimpled, naked toddler
wrapped in black, velvet space,
belly and face glowing

toward one another,
wave and particle
like twin moons.

POEM IN WHICH I EVENTUALLY
ROCK TO WHITMAN

Crew teams, a singlet or so, turn
the water's weight, river sparking
silver shards, as if to coxswains'
drumbeat. We're walking, stopping

to rest Dawn's new back, now housing
hardware: six screws, two rods held
in place by bone harvested from
her hip. Arriving in Philadelphia

in 1892 from a village in Russia,
Simon Klein opened the grocery store
where this October afternoon in 2024
we purchase root vegetables pulled

from Jersey soil for tonight's soup.
The day's all rhythm, all back and
forth, the river turning, our walking,
our minds dipping through centuries

like oars pushing and pulling.
At the next resting spot, cradling
a few pounds of parsnips swaddled
in brown paper, I start to sway,

begin, without intent, a mother's
rock I've witnessed women perform
around babies' cries for closeness,
milk. Dawn stands to go on as I

go on rocking the parsnips
like a nanny, curious, suddenly,
as to why this indoor/outdoor
bar's named *Bishop's Collar,*

know that I can rock the parsnips
with one arm, Google with another
to learn that this term refers to
the head on a Guinness, white foam

atop dark ale like the circling
white band above Catholic
bishops' black frocks, like a
river's froth, all of me wanting

all of it together, synchronized
rowing, Klein's supermarket,
babies held, fed, full, harvests
of enough, flesh fixed with

bionics, death, of course, death,
bishops blessing whomever
we love to go on and on, cradling
earth, seas, endlessly rocking.

ODE TO THE DEKOPON

A one-pound globe,
its severed stem
a five-point star.
Feel it between
your hands—
its tough topknot,
bumps and grooves
like a brain. Even unpeeled,
it lowers my blood pressure
like lakes, wilderness.
Oh, wedding of pebbled skin
with lace of white pith.
Coupling of squat sumo body
and oozing, sweet crescents.
Precious citrus:
$3.99 for one,
a bougie exile from
the hip, democratic thingness
of American poetics.
So I celebrate
the dekopon here.
Just as I justify
its price tag with the labor
of bringing it to be.
Grafted, cloned, hybridized—
it takes two years for
its flower to form.

My mother recalled
citrus Christmases
during the Great Depression,
watching grocers balance
Florida's juicy orbs,
stack them in store windows,
Salvation Army bells
ringing Hosannas.
This March morning at Aldi's,
piles of luscious seedless
Sumos beckon, lure strands
of winter-weary shoppers
to gather, together.

III

GATHERERS

I
On the road to Evora,
goldfinches sail miles
of olive orchards, filch
fields of sunflower seed.
I figure the winged set piece
for this day's done when
dozens of stork nests
sized like kids' pup tents
tangle in trees, atop electricity
poles, empty, it seems, before
parents rise slowly, sentries
framing cloudless sky blue as blade,
necks thin white steeples,
then horizontal arrows in flight
headed to marsh. When their
black-edged pinions unfurl,
my throat opens to cry out
for their return, tastes twisting
minnows from their mouths
as they funnel that salty sweet
stew into nestlings' throats.

II
Evora's Capela dos Ossos
greets the living thusly:

"We bones that here are,
for yours await." I face skulls
patinaed by centuries, walls
of plastered crossbones in artful
symmetry, finally find the backstory:
when Black Death had its way twice
in two centuries with human beings,
starvation followed plague
as cemeteries ate up farmland.
Franciscan monks turned saviors,
found sacred industry exhuming
graveyards, carting skeletons to this church
as *memento mori* art, then planting crops
in loam enriched by human bodies.

MOTHERS AND THIEVES

In the room the women come and go
Talking of Michelangelo.
"The Love Song of J. Alfred Prufrock"

Below *The Creation of Adam*
fresco, we lift our eyes toward
a cloud-clotted ceiling. Amid
the crowd's hive hum, the guards'
shouts for quiet, a small woman
appears beside me, edging closer
in this stifling space, wearing
her backpack fronted like a baby
carrier, cushioning me from her
pushing bodily intimacy.
I try to draw my personal bubble.
Still, she seeks my ear, blurts:
"Where's the famous one?"
I stretch my index finger high
above my head as if trying to insert
my own pointer into God and Adam's
trembling force field, touch
my pooched mouth, librarian-like,
to invite silence. But she must speak,
stitches her story to me in patches
of pain: "Pickpocket . . . passport . . .
felt a tug on my pack . . . pregnant
girl . . . how could a mother . . . ?" I can't

look away from her. I can't not sketch
the thief's portrait in my head—young,
flip-flopped feet swollen with heat
and child, her eyes focused, searching.
The museum is closing. I have missed
my minutes to muse on Adam's bulging
thighs, Eve's startling pubescence,
her naked vulnerability moments after
God created her, hands clasped perhaps
in gratitude, certainly in supplication.
I want to know why Michelangelo
made God crowded in a scarlet shell
the texture and shape of a uterus, snuggled
there with cherubim, seraphim, a woman.
Less meta: why has God the He cribbed
a woman's womb to create the first man?
Am I looking at the high Renaissance
or Judy Chicago's "Dinner Party"?
I turn to the woman who robbed me
of my Sistine Chapel moments. But
she's gone—stolen from me.

WINTER

when Wolf Moon

pulled us to snow-layered hills
                    packs of Sisyphus littles
trudge back up backup back
        up back up back
        up
            howling down hard-packed freeze

    rolling off sleds snow pants swishing

    breath pepperminted steam frothing

                    our chapped faces.

I knew how to steer
            some,

    but not to brake

    highway traffic cutting across our sledding street

    might slice through us

                    whooshing quiet fast and low
in the gloaming

but never did.

The only girl on a Flying Saucer

disappeared

on her walk home from

school one Friday.

We joined the search for her

under

Hunger Moon

PEARLS

When our mom pierced
her ears in her middle
years, her Christmas
stocking held a silver
foiled box of cultured
pearl studs she asked
my father for and wore
until decades later,
when sticking metal
through her lobes while
meds thinned her blood
could double as a crime scene.

Mom was left with
the singular art of
decking dresses with
the pearl necklace
Dad bought for her
as a schoolgirl. Until
I, wanting to change
the worn cord, secure
a catch her palsied hands
might manage, rescue
the flimsy strand for repair.

The jeweler lifts the
necklace from its plush

box, tooths the beads, whispers
"Synthetic—do you still
want to spend the money?"
I nod, wondering, even,
if they "could bleach
the yellowed plastic?"

I'm longing, though she
rarely did, for a posher thing,
labor turned to luxury:
oyster white pearls formed
from sandy accretion,
shining globes hatched
as protection, adaptation—
like the girl, raised with
live-in maids, who married
down, made our clothes,
our cakes and quilts,
made do for decades,
happy, she claimed,
as a clam.

I LOST THE WORD FLEECE

felt its retrieval might
take hours, maybe a day,
as did *turnip* from last month,
appearing suddenly as I rattled
around in a refrigerator drawer
searching for fennel. When
my hand landed on that
chunky root vegetable,
I shouted with the eureka
ecstasy of an astrophysicist
finding a new galaxy.

But the word *fleece* acted like
a travel writer touring the stretch
of West Indies, soaking in
the sun of each white sandy
beach or swimming pool
from the Bahamas to Barbados,
emailing their editor that
the assignment needed more
time, its storyline swelling
with each dripping, Creamsicle
sunset. Yes—the word *fleece*
took its time, as if the object itself,
overworked and underpaid for
its warming comfort, needed
a long rest, a neat whiskey

in front of a fireplace tucked away
in the Adirondacks.

I tried to give the word *fleece*
that mountain vacation. But I grew
impatient. I decided to lure the word
to the thing itself by wearing it,
pushed my head through the blue
sweater-jacket, pulled tight its zipper,
walked about silently,
inviting the word, like a long absent,
migrating Monarch, to land on me,
a fir forest in the highlands of Mexico.

Days passed. This morning, folding
laundry, stacking t-shirts with Marie
Kondo semi-joy, I sensed the
labiodental fricative "fl" struggling
against my mouth to escape. "*Fleece!*,"
I cried out, cradling myself, my fleecy
arms, as if I had given birth to
human language.

ON WALKING RICHMOND'S MONUMENT AVENUE

Nov. 1, 2022

White-on-white marble pedestals, naked
as newborns, gleam in afternoon sun. Stripped
of status, Stonewall Jackson, Jefferson Davis
now gone to ground, statues shrouded in black
tarp at Richmond's wastewater storage plant
for repurpose, not like, but with, human shit.
America: let's not upcycle Civil War cronies
back into palatable fare. Been done. Our neo-
Nazis still busy at it. Let's look long at this
once-upon-a-time capital of the Confederacy,
this avenue lined with mansions, magnolias,
bones of our enslaved. At last, let's unmyth
white supremacy. On this Day of the Dead,
what glorious emptiness we are called to fill.

ON DISTINGUISHING BETWEEN POLITICAL SYSTEMS OVER SUSHI WITH MY FIRST SON AND GRANDSON

When the edamame lands among us, my son and I
chart the rise of autocracies, the decline of global liberal
democracies in this century, while Adrian, eyeing the just-
delivered Seaweed Salad, questions the difference between
"just plain and liberal democracy," so Jon and I talk over
Sashimi and one another. I perform a seminar in roots and
prefixes, defining the Greek stem "cracy" before mixing
and matching auto-, pluto-, demos- and merito-, illustrate
by moving fishy prefixes—Spicy Yellowfin and Spider Roll
pieces—on to the Dragon Roll base. My son discourses
on voting rights, threats to representative democracy, so
I abandon my less-than-sexy seminar, say yes to another
glass of white wine, no to dessert. Adrian switches it up
to talk about AirPods and Air Jordan Retro Fire Reds
before we walk the block to his sisters' Community Center
Play, *The Most Epic Birthday Party*, in which a fifth-grade,
erstwhile populist leader becomes a dictator overnight,
replete with crown and scepter. Adrian raises his eyebrows,
tosses his head to the stage, whispers "prefix: auto, the root,
cracy." For our next sushi night: how autocracy happened
here.

A LEAF IS BOTH A THING AND A PROCESS

Ironing fall's fallen
churched me early
that death could even

trick itself. I'd peel
orange & red pin oak
& maple hands from

wax paper gloves, wedge
our ironing board back
between washer & wall,

tuck the leaves into manila
sleeves bound for third-grade
glory. Our desks gobbled

with turkeys traced from fingers
& a thumb. Brown construction
tree trunks & branches alive

with kids' pressed bright death
flashed on our art board. What
did we know of the biochemistry

behind dark & cold's russet matter?
These mornings when I wake
I'm still startled by my silver

crown, crepiness in my arms' flesh,
grinding in my knee bones, still
wishing for the wand of elementary art.

AFTER

my decade's renunciation, again with
their glitter, gaiety, ball-dropping countdown.
A drunk girl gives demure, bends to offer

champagne Jello shots on a silver tray, plastic
gold cups shimmering, wobbling with her décolletage.

Each December, this late lust for transformation.
Dry Januarys, freezing sea dunks, grown
children divorcing their parents like detox.

      Let's lose the bent old man handing his car keys
      to a diapered baby in top hat—so on repeat, so stale.

      Nothing will do now but metamorphoses.

      Let's slip our skin this New Year,
                        change our species.

I'll lead, follow my fear, drop to the floor, slither across
hardwood to the tree, rake my back on its piney bark,
my tongue licking air, then sneak bluish into a kitchen

drawer, scrape knife's edge for my peel, shed brittle coils
to spook our host hunting for morning coffee spoons.

Four tall, lean ladies, wrapped in black pleather,
silk scarves riding their bare arms, press to the end
of a time-lapse video, crawl new from chrysalis,

flap their wet shine of wings, orange fans circled,
segmented with black, their dozens of legs shaky

as new foals.

We've changed.

              Though we can't live a day in this cold and dark.

I've missed October's brumation: warm curls
of us who wake, wriggle away to sip melted ice,
swallow stunned mice, return to wrap together

 beneath stone.

And those flitting females skipped fall's Mexican
migration, hardly a vacation, sailing thousands of sky
miles to eat, mate in heat, drop pearly, spring eggs.

How to survive, to continue?

Again, transform: be charmed back to human—
repaired, hopeful, perhaps even happy
for a time in our soiled, sweet, sorrowful living.

"CATERPILLAR

will be your friend," quips the
dermatologist, sewing a squiggly
incision up my lower left cheek.
We'd rehearsed his sequence: scrape
out my cancered tissue, lay layers on
the microscope lens, return to dig
a deeper well in my face, finish
when he finds flesh clean of carcinoma
cells, finally whipstitch the wound,
pressuring epidermal bumps to rise,
segmented larva now wiggling,
fuzzy with snipped tufts of thread,
cocooned in white gauze,
waiting

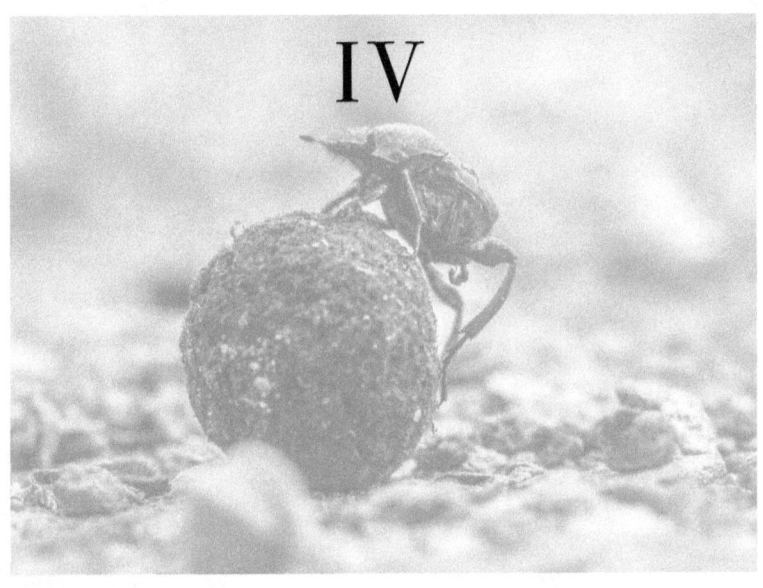

IV

ON EVOLUTIONARY ADAPTABILITY:
A CHTHULUCENE SONNET CROWN

ULYSSES ALSO STEERED BY THE NIGHT SKY

Some dung beetles navigate by the stars,
rolling their multivalent ball by night,
Milky Way snapshots stored in their brains.
Hatching from an egg inside their brood balls,

larvae's poop-packed lunch lasts for days.
Dung dudes proffer these piles like champagne
and oysters: coat in pheromones, position
near tunnels of love, wait for partners,

their butts lifting in lust, cooling post-coital
in these earthen globes. A poem, really,
this stunning compression, this roving ball
of Tinder, birth, nourishment, home—net zero,

too, I muse, roaming my domestic sphere,
sprawling rooms of human being.

THE COMFORT INN

Sprawling rooms of human being,
volleyball squads stretch across the Inn's
entrance, cluster like stands of Sequoias
bending toward TV, each other, grabbing

fists of pizza from a table's tower
of boxes. Tomorrow's the tourney, Penn
players tell me, as they lope down dark plaid
hallways, elevator up to bed, warm and full.

Comfort finds me this night on white pillows
mounded like clean snow, dreams tumbling
deep and long. I wake to worry about my
son, team star turned to phobias, addiction.

I rise, drive a narrow road to state prison,
morning glowing rose gold on winter trees.

THE PAST MAKING ITSELF PRESENT
IN THE FUTURE

Morning glowing rose gold on winter trees,
I greet dawn deep breathing, name gratitude

out loud. When sun throws Geometry's shapes
on wall and floor, I practice new angles:

downward dog longer, faster my walks, less
is more my closet, revise like a boss.

Let's mark our days with ceremony:
braise leeks and lamb with rosemary, magic

stoops with pansies in pots, praise Polaris
before you sleep, kiss your love, plant milkweed

mornings for Monarchs to feed, call gray wolves
to mountains and forests, sing whale in dreams.

Some of this will vanish. Though I want what lasts.
Sonnet's response: this form, these lines, the past.

THE INTRICACY AND UTILITY
OF WINGED CREATURES

Sonnets' response: this form, these lines, the past.
Can Anthropocene conceits, poetry,
outlast nature? Nah. Let's look again
at insects. A giant lacewing, thought extinct

since the Age of Aquarius in North
America, clung to a Walmart's wall
in Arkansas, the searchlight an
entomologist's eye. Their pale gray larvae

sport long mandibles like tiny alligators
to scissor prey, stab aphids, slurp nectar.
Hanging here since Jurassic's Age—now that's
endurance. Sapiens' 160,000 years, Moon landing

notwithstanding, seem a blurb, a blip beside
winged creatures greening gardens, lasting.

MORE LIFE

Winged creatures greening gardens, lasting;
an endless summer idyll from my childhood
book of fairied tales. Let's adult our myths,

turn to modernity, science, living
longer: our human lifespan doubled
in a single century. Now most of us

live to 73. Thank science—
human adaptation's source and result:
sewers, vaccines, antibiotics. Add

refrigeration, chlorination. But
longer human life birthed our planet's
dying. Will we scrub sky's carbon

to cool Earth's frying, rejig the future?
Adaptation's policy, not poetry.

THE BACK AND FORTH OF THINGS

Adaptation's policy, not poetry.
Seems an argument for art's extinction,
fiddling while Rome burns and all of that.

Science saves and destroys us, what's left
to say? What for, these lines and lasting?

Though I've forgotten names of lovers,
Hopkins' "Nothing is so beautiful as
spring—When weeds in wheels, shoot long and lovely

and lush" has stayed. I want the world
to open windows, whoosh poetry in
like April air, lungs lush with language,

bodies' rhythm sprung, hearts pumping
with metaphor's grace—
to make new things both disparate, the same.

GREEN DREAM VISION

To make new things both disparate, the same,
my blonde boy, age 8, joins his shaved head
man-self, released just now from prison, and me,
so many ages all at once, in our farm's
switchgrass field. Stalks reach to our waists and chests,
tickling our arms, scratching our noses, hundreds
of green grasshoppers jumping and spitting
around us, their babies dotting slender leaves
like pea-green pencil points. We find Matt's
rusty bug boxes in the barn, filled with mantis,
hungry, kneeling, so the boy frees them,
the man blesses them. Nightfall we lie
in dewed green liberty, begin the story:
some dung beetles navigate by the stars.

NOTES

"Wave Field" is after Maya Lin's installation, Storm King Arts Center, Hudson Valley, New York.

"Each Other" is indebted to Edgar Kunz's poem "Tuning," which it intentionally echoes in structure and theme.

"Grindavík, Iceland" is an ekphrastic poem after "Fish Drying," Jon Gunnarsson, oil painting, 1980.

"Ode to the Dekopon" was inspired by and follows a structure akin to Ellen Bass' "Ode to the First Peach."

I borrow the title "A Leaf is Both a Thing and a Process," from writer Chris Abani. He used this phrase in an online guest talk he delivered for Ellen Bass' *Living Room Craft Talks, Series 5*, in the Fall of 2022.

In "Caravaggio's Lightboxes," I refer to two sources that engage with the objects in the poem's title. One occurs in Anthony Doerr's *Four Seasons in Rome (2007)*, when he recounts how Caravaggio's *Crucifixion of St. Peter* in the church of Santa Maria del Popolo appeared an indecipherable canvas of black and maroon until another visitor used a coin-operated lightbox to illuminate it. The other is from Eithne Longstaff's online *Rattle* poem, "My Wife, Sewing at a Window," another Roman Caravaggio moment, in which the speaker clattered coins in a metal box to brighten a Caravaggio.

I owe the title "Poem in Which I Eventually Rock to Whitman" to Denise Duhamel's prize-winning *Rattle* chapbook *In Which*.

I borrow the term "Chthulucene" included in the end-of-collection sonnet crown from Donna. J. Haraway. A feminist, multispecies environmental philosopher and author of *Staying with the Trouble: Making Kin in the Chthulucene,* Haraway decenters sapiens from Earth's living species. She theorizes that adaptability to climate change has, will, and must involve a compost pile of multiple-species interactions. I am indebted to NPR"s *Skywatch* for some of the information in "Ulysses Also Steered by the Night Sky."

I also borrow the title "The Past Making Itself Present in the Future" for the third sonnet in the crown from the Pulitzer Winning novel *Trust*, by Hernandez Diaz.

My source for the winged creature in the fourth sonnet of that crown is a digital *New York Times* article. "'What Is This Thing?': How a Jurassic-Era Insect Was Rediscovered in a Walmart," March 2, 2023.

ACKNOWLEDGMENTS

I thank the editors of the following publications in which these poems, some in different forms, or bearing different titles, first appeared:

After Happy Hour: "How I Dream About Climate Change"

Big City Lit: "Chaos Theory"

Crab Creek Review: "Wave Field"

Ekphrastic Review: "Grindavik, Iceland"

Ginosko Literary Journal: "History with Jehovah's Witnesses," "Winter," "Before I Knew about Breakfast at Tiffany's," and "Caterpillar"

Gyroscope Review: "On Distinguishing Between Political Systems Over Sushi with My First Son and Grandson"

Illuminations: "On Visiting My Son in a State Correctional Institute," and "On Walking Richmond's Monument Avenue"

MacQueen's Quinterly: "Peaches," "Ukrainian Easter Eggs," "Pearls"

Naugatuck River Review: "Mother Never Smoked"

Quartet: "When Hayden Carruth Visited My High School Creative Writing Class"

Third Wednesday: "Elegy for a Majorette" and "Poem in Which I Eventually Rock to Whitman"

West Trade Review's Iron Oak Editions anthology *Eco Blooms: Poetry at the Intersection of Social Identity and Nature/Environment/Place:* "Each Other"

Willows Wept Review: "I Have Not Been Able to Write the Lake Ontario Poem," "Moon Jellies," and "On Evolutionary Adaptability: A Sonnet Crown"

GRATITUDE

My Zoom writing group workshops kept my writing practice on its toes and kibbitzing about poems and poetics during the evolution of this collection. Heartfelt thanks to Mary Rohrer-Dann, Dawn Terpstra, and Robbin Farr.

Immense gratitude to the staff at Green Writers Press, particularly to publisher extraordinaire Dede Cummings as well as to Megan Buchanan and Ramona Boyd-Foley for their shrewd editing.

Thanks to Moonstone Arts Center and Bucknell's Stadler Center for Poetry and the Literary Arts through which I could share poems while working on this collection.

I am deeply grateful to my partner and poetic arbiter, William Keeney, with whom I daily share my poetry, life, and love.

Special and deep gratitude and hugs to my former student, dear friend, and publicist, Allison Berger Hartman, whose social media expertise and beautiful spirit have enhanced my work's digital presence and endeared her to a variety of audiences.

www.ingramcontent.com/pod-product-compliance
Lightning Source LLC
Chambersburg PA
CBHW020756130626
46554CB00006B/2217